The Life and World of

FLORENCE NIGHTINGALE

Struan Reid

Heinemann
LIBRARY

www.heinemann/library.co.uk
Visit our website to find out more information about Heinemann Library books.

To order:
 Phone 44 (0) 1865 888066
 Send a fax to 44 (0) 1865 314091
Visit the Heinemann Library Bookshop at www.heinemann/library.co.uk to browse our catalogue and order online.

First published in Great Britain by Heinemann Library, Halley Court, Jordan Hill, Oxford OX2 8EJ, part of Harcourt Education. Heinemann is a registered trademark of Harcourt Education Ltd.

Editorial: Lucy Thunder and Helen Cox
Design: Ron Kamen and Celia Floyd
Illustrations: Jeff Edwards and Joanna Brooker
Picture Research: Rebecca Sodergren and Elaine Willis
Production: Séverine Ribierre

Originated by Ambassador Litho Ltd
Printed and bound in China by W K T

ISBN 978 0 431 14782 6 (HB)
07 06 05 04 03
10 9 8 7 6 5 4 3 2 1

ISBN 978 0 431 14789 5 (PB)
09
10 9 8 7 6 5 4

British Library Cataloguing in Publication Data
Reid, Struan
Life and world of Florence Nightingale
610.7'3'092

A full catalogue record for this book is available from the British Library.

Acknowledgements
The Publishers would like to thank the following for permission to reproduce photographs:
AKG p. **16**; Art Archive p. **9**; Bridgeman Art Library pp. **14** (Collection of the Earl of Pembroke, Wilton House, Wiltshire), **18** (Private Collection), **20**, **23** (Greater London Council); British Library p. **7**; Corbis pp. **6**, **29** (Peter Saloutos); Florence Nightingale Museum pp. **8**, **22**, **24**, **25**; Fotomas p. **21**; Hulton Getty p. **4**; Hulton Deutsch Collection/Corbis p. **28**; Illustrated London News p. **19**; Mary Evans Picture Library pp. **10**, **11**; National Army Museum p. **27**; National Portrait Gallery p. **13**; National Trust p. **26**; Peter Newark p. **12**; Wellcome Trust pp. **15**, **17**.

Cover photograph of Florence Nightingale, reproduced with permission of Hulton Archives.

The Publishers would like to thank Rebecca Vickers for her assistance in the preparation of this book.

Every effort has been made to contact copyright holders of any material reproduced in this book. Any omissions will be rectified in subsequent printings if notice is given to the Publishers.

Contents

Any words shown in the text in bold, **like this**, are explained in the Glossary.

Who was Florence Nightingale?

Florence Nightingale is one of the most famous women in British history. She was born in 1820 into a rich and privileged family, and she spent much of her life **campaigning** to improve the treatment of poor and sick people in Britain and other parts of the world. She fought to improve **public health services**, and founded the Nightingale Training School for Nurses, which laid the foundations for nursing today.

Changing attitudes

Florence was a very brave and determined woman who became famous for leading a group of nurses during the **Crimean War** of 1853–56. She changed the way military hospitals were run and wounded soldiers were treated.

Florence Nightingale lived during the Victorian age, when Victoria was Queen and Britain was the richest and most powerful nation in the world. This was an age when women, and especially women from her privileged background, were not expected to work. Through her hard work she changed society's attitudes to women.

▶ **This photograph of Florence Nightingale was taken in 1856, when she was 37 years old. She was already one of the most famous people in England.**

4

◀ This map shows the position of the Crimea peninsula and the hospital at Scutari where Florence Nightingale first became famous.

How do we know?

Florence Nightingale wrote hundreds of letters to her family, friends and politicians, and many of them have survived. They give us valuable information about her life and work and the times in which she lived. She also kept a diary. This was found recently after being lost and forgotten for many years. It contains more detailed information about her thoughts, daily life and the people she met. There were also many newspaper articles written about Florence Nightingale.

Key dates

1820	Florence Nightingale is born
1845	Florence wants to train as a nurse but her family stop her
1851	Florence works at the Kaiserswerth Institute in Germany
1853	Florence is appointed **Superintendent** at a hospital
1854	Florence leads a team of nurses during the Crimean War
1856	Florence returns to England when peace is declared
1860	The Nightingale Training School for Nurses opens
1907	Florence is awarded the **Order of Merit**
1910	Florence Nightingale dies

A future heroine

Florence Nightingale was born on 12 May 1820. She was the second child of William and Fanny Nightingale. They had married two years earlier and had travelled to Italy for a long **honeymoon**. Their first child, a girl named Parthenope, was born in the southern Italian city of Naples in 1819. Florence was named after the northern Italian city where she was born.

Wealthy parents

William Nightingale was a very wealthy man who owned large **estates** in Derbyshire and Hampshire. He was the son of a successful banker and mine-owner and he had also **inherited** a fortune from an uncle. He was a shy and quiet man who was rich enough not to have to work. This allowed him to pursue his main interests of reading and studying. His wife, Fanny Nightingale, was six years older. She was much more lively than her husband and enjoyed going to parties and entertaining at the family homes.

▲ The city of Florence, in Italy. This was the favourite city of Florence's parents, and the place after which they named her.

A leisurely routine

When the Nightingales and their two young daughters returned to England from Italy, they settled into a very comfortable life. For most of the year the family lived at Embley House, a large home in the New Forest in Hampshire. Fanny's two sisters lived in the area and Florence, her mother and sister would often spend their time visiting their relations and friends.

Once or twice a year, the family travelled to London. This was always very exciting. Once in London, Fanny would entertain guests and she loved to go to other people's parties and to the theatre. During the summer months, Florence and her family travelled north to stay at their house in Derbyshire, called Lea Hurst.

◀ **This photograph shows William Nightingale in his old age.**

Raising children

Florence Nightingale and her sister Parthenope had everything they needed. However, for most children growing up in England at that time, life was very different. Poor families often had very little to eat. Children could suffer from terrible illnesses such as **rickets** and **influenza** because of their poor diet and the cold, damp buildings in which they lived. Many of them died in infancy, and mothers often died in childbirth.

Growing up in comfort

Florence and Parthenope, or Flo and Parthe as they were known in the family, were given all the toys and comforts that money could buy. They were dressed in beautiful clothes and they were invited to parties given by their cousins and other friends. They had pets like kittens and puppies to play with, went for walks in the beautiful gardens at Embley House and rode on ponies in the park. Their mother had 2 sisters and 8 brothers, and altogether Florence and Parthenope had 27 cousins!

Lessons at home

From about the age of four, Flo and Parthe were taught by a **governess**. They learned about British history and geography, and read exciting stories. They were also taught French and German. When they were twelve and thirteen years old, their father started to teach them. Every morning they would go down to the library at Embley House where their father would be sitting behind his enormous wooden desk. He gave them lessons in French, German and Italian, and taught them Latin and ancient Greek. They continued their lessons in history and geography, and also started studying **philosophy**.

▲ This drawing of Embley House – the Nightingale family home – was done by Parthenope.

Two different characters

Florence really enjoyed these lessons with her father. She was quiet and studious, just like him, and she was very intelligent and quick to learn. Parthenope did not enjoy the daily lessons nearly as much. She began to grow jealous of her sister and the way she was so good at her studies. When Parthenope was sixteen, she was so unhappy that she persuaded her mother to take her out of the classes and to give her flower arranging and music lessons instead. She was now much happier, but she was still very jealous of her sister.

▲ The cities of England grew rapidly throughout the nineteenth century, as more and more people flocked to them to work in the factories.

The Industrial Revolution

Florence grew up at a time when the Industrial Revolution was changing the face of Europe. It was a period when traditional **industries** such as weaving were transformed by the invention of machinery powered by steam and water. Britain became the richest country in the world, although only a small handful of people enjoyed the incredible wealth that was created. Hundreds of thousands of others moved from the countryside into the expanding cities to work in huge factories. Many lived in terrible conditions, working like slaves to operate new machines.

Longing for more

When Florence Nightingale was growing up, young ladies like her were expected to marry rich young men, raise a family and support their husbands. Fanny Nightingale had done this for her husband, and she expected her daughters to do the same.

Training for marriage

Florence loved reading and spent as much time as she could in her father's library. However, she was growing into a very beautiful young lady. While she continued her lessons with her father, she was also expected to learn other, more 'useful' skills that would win her a husband. She was expected to sit with her mother and sister when friends came to visit, to dress well, look pretty and hold light, amusing conversations.

Tired of parties

Parthenope may have enjoyed doing these things, but Florence did not. She soon grew tired of the endless parties, the dressing up and the talking. She had often seen poor families struggling to survive in the countryside round Embley House and Lea Hurst. She had seen girls and boys her own age begging for food and money with no shoes on. There must be something she could do to help them.

▶ A sketch of Florence as a young woman. She spent much of her time reading books in her father's library.

When Florence was sixteen, something very strange happened to her. 'On 7 February 1837, God spoke to me and called me to His service.' She wrote this many years later, but until then she had told no one about her feelings. She did not know at that time what it was she was supposed to do, but she hoped that one day everything would fall into place.

◀ Queen Victoria was the same age as Florence. Later, she admired Florence's work and would give her much support.

Queen Victoria

Queen Victoria was born in 1819. She became queen in 1837, at the age of only eighteen, when her uncle, King William IV, died. She was also head of the British Empire. She reigned for 64 years until 1901. Her reign was so long and so successful that the period is now known as the Victorian age. Queen Victoria was followed on the British throne by her son, King Edward VII.

A wider world

In 1837, soon after Florence's strange experience, she and her family left England for a tour of Europe. On 8 September, the family and six servants climbed into horse-drawn coaches and set off from Embley House for the coast, where they boarded a boat to France. They would be away for a year and a half.

New horizons

Florence was thrilled to be going as she knew that her whole world would open up and she would see many interesting places and people. The Nightingales travelled through France and Switzerland, and on to Italy. They toured the lakes in the north of the country and stayed in the city of Florence where they went to concerts and the opera, museums and art galleries.

Florence and her family arrived back in England in April 1839. From April until July, they stayed in London with one of Fanny's sisters and her family. Once again, Florence felt that she was wasting her time and she wanted to do more. When the family moved north to Lea Hurst in Derbyshire, Florence started taking food and medicines to poor and sick people living nearby. At least this work made her feel useful.

◄ Florence (sitting) and her sister Parthenope. There was a lot of rivalry between the two sisters when they were young, but later they became firm friends.

An offer of marriage

In 1842, when Florence was 22, she met a well-known **journalist** called Richard Monckton Milnes. He was a very intelligent and sensitive man and Florence liked him very much. Some months later, Richard asked her to marry him. Although she was very attracted to Richard, Florence felt that she was not yet ready to marry and settle down to the sort of life her mother expected of her. And so she asked Richard to wait before she gave her answer, until she was sure what she wanted to do.

▶ This portrait of the journalist Richard Monckton Milnes was completed in about 1844, two years after he and Florence first met.

Dutiful wives

Women in Victorian times were expected to marry and to entirely devote their lives to their husbands. Whether they were rich or poor, women were all expected to have children and to run the family home. If they did go out to work, they were expected to give all the money they earned to their husbands. Any woman who was well-educated was regarded with suspicion.

A change of life

By the time Florence Nightingale was 24, she was growing more and more certain that she wanted to help sick people. In 1845, she asked her parents if she could train to be a nurse at the hospital in Salisbury, a city in Wiltshire not far from Embley House.

Sent away

Florence's parents were shocked – they were not expecting their daughter to work at all, let alone as a nurse! In desperation, Florence tried to learn all she could about medicine and nursing in secret in her own time. This secrecy and hard work made Florence very ill and, at the end of 1847, she was on the edge of having a **nervous breakdown**.

In 1847, two family friends called Charles and Selina Bracebridge took Florence away with them for a holiday in Italy. Florence was now 27, and her parents hoped that the holiday would finally change her mind and make her settle down and get married. However, it had the opposite effect and made her even more determined to go into nursing. She spent six months in Rome, where she met a rich Englishman called Sidney Herbert. He encouraged her to pursue a career as a nurse.

▶ **Florence's friend Sidney Herbert became an influential politician and Florence's greatest champion.**

Making decisions

Florence returned to England, strong and determined. She wrote to Richard Monckton Milnes and thanked him for his offer of marriage. She told him that she could not accept as she would be unable to be a good wife and a good nurse at the same time. She also told her parents that from now on she would devote herself to nursing. They were very upset by this news. 'It was if I had wanted to be a kitchen-maid', she was to write years later.

▶ As this drawing shows, at the time Florence was trying to become a nurse, most women working in nursing were considered to be drunken layabouts.

Nursing

Nursing at this time was regarded as a very poor job, and certainly not one fit for a 'lady'. Women who worked as nurses were expected to be like servants – changing beds, cooking, lighting fires, washing patients and so on. Many people believed that most nurses were **drunkards**, lazy and inefficient. This is an unfair picture as many of them were very hard-working and caring. However, it is true that most of them knew very little about medicine or **hygiene**.

Nurse Nightingale

Florence's parents and sister still kept trying to put her off the idea of working as a nurse. Once more, they sent her away on holiday hoping that she would forget about these silly ideas. This time she went with the Bracebridges on a cruise round the Mediterranean, visiting Italy, Greece and Egypt.

Finding her feet

On their way back to England in July 1850, they travelled through Germany where Florence had time to visit the Kaiserswerth Institute. There, women from rich families often worked as nurses. Florence was so impressed by their work that she was even more determined that this was what she would do herself.

When she returned home, Florence's father realized that nothing would change his daughter's mind. In 1851, when Florence was 31, he agreed to let her go and work at the Kaiserswerth Institute for three months. She was thrilled when she started working there as she felt that at last she was doing something useful with her life. She got up at five o'clock every morning and her working day was very hard and tiring. Florence had never been happier.

▲ This is a picture of the Kaiserswerth Institute near Dusseldorf. It was originally established as a religious foundation to aid the sick and the poor, and the daughters of rich German families often went there to help.

▲ When Florence started work as a nurse, most hospitals were very badly run. There were never enough doctors and nurses to treat the patients, and the wards were usually very dirty.

Father's support

By now, William Nightingale was very impressed by his daughter's determination and he began to support her plans for becoming a nurse. Against the wishes of his wife, he backed Florence when, in 1853, she was appointed **Superintendent** of the Institute for the Care of Sick Gentlewomen in London. This was a very important job and Florence was taken on to reorganize completely the running of the Institute. William was very proud of her and gave her an allowance (money) so that she could afford to live comfortably in London on her own. At last, at the age of 33 and after many years of fighting with her family, Florence was making a life of her own.

Victorian hospitals

At the time when Florence started working at the Institute for the Care of Sick Gentlewomen in London, hospitals were not very well organized. There were usually far too few doctors and nurses to treat the sick. Florence quickly realized that the nursing staff at her hospital needed reorganizing. They needed proper training so that they knew about medicines and **hygiene** and how to work together as a team.

War in the Crimea

In 1853, not long after Florence Nightingale started working in London, the **Crimean War** broke out between Russia and Turkey. Russia tried to take control of a huge sea between the two countries, called the Black Sea, and also parts of Turkish **territory** in eastern Europe. In March 1854, Britain and France sent soldiers to support the Turkish Army.

Unprepared

The commanders of the British Army sent to help the Turks were totally unprepared for the terrible conditions they found when they arrived. The British soldiers sailed to the Turkish port of Scutari on the southern coast of the Black Sea. Within the first week of their arrival, the soldiers were dying in their hundreds from an outbreak of **cholera**. Soon, one thousand men had died from the disease, and this was before any fighting had even taken place.

▲ British soldiers fighting Russians in the Crimean War. Many soldiers died in the fighting, but many more died from disease.

Weak and exhausted

Many of the surviving soldiers were very weak, cold and hungry. They were crammed into ships and sent across the Black Sea to the Crimean Peninsula in Russia. Even though they were so weak and ill, they attacked and drove the Russian Army back into a city called Sebastopol. The fighting that followed lasted nearly a year, and many soldiers on both sides died. About 21,000 British soldiers were killed, and of those over three quarters died from cholera.

No help

There were few medicines to treat the soldiers as these had been left behind at Scutari. So the wounded soldiers were bundled on to ships and sent back across the Black Sea. When they arrived in Scutari, the doctors there were still struggling to cope with the cholera outbreak and the army hospitals were in chaos.

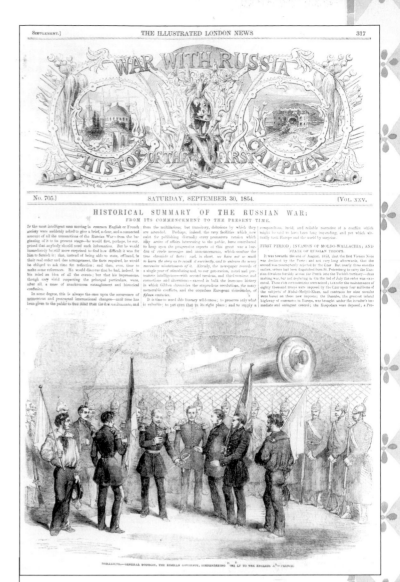

▲ This newspaper article of September 1854 is discussing the Crimean War. At first people were in favour of sending troops to fight the Russians, but they were shocked when they read reports of the fighting.

Dying from disease

Cholera is a terrible disease that is caused by **bacteria** called *Vibria cholerae*. A person can catch it by drinking water or eating food that has been infected by the bacteria. If it is not treated immediately, cholera can kill a person within a matter of hours. Cholera also broke out several times in Britain from 1832 onwards. In 1849, for example, one outbreak killed as many as 13,000 people in London alone.

Wartime nurses

When Britain entered the **Crimean War**, Florence Nightingale had been running the hospital in London for just a year. In that time she had made many changes to the way it functioned. She had sacked some of the old staff and some of the others had chosen to leave. After only a short time, she had transformed the hospital into a very efficient organization.

Shocking news

While Florence was working in London, the situation in the Crimea was getting worse and worse. A **journalist** called William Russell had travelled out to the Crimea and started sending back reports about the British soldiers dying from disease, cold and hunger. Sidney Herbert, Florence's old friend from Rome, was now Secretary of War in the British government and, like many other people at the time, he was shocked when he read Russell's reports in the newspapers.

▲ This nurse is treating a wounded soldier near a Crimean battlefield in 1855. The nurses, who went out near the fighting, were incredibly brave and had to face great danger.

On 15 October 1854, Sidney Herbert wrote to Florence to ask for her help. She agreed and, at the age of 34, was made **Superintendent** of the Nursing Establishment in Turkey. This time, even Florence's mother and sister supported her. Parthe wrote: 'It is a great and noble work.' Florence put together a group of 38 nurses to help her. After sixteen days at sea, they arrived at Scutari and travelled to the British military hospital nearby.

Terrible conditions

Nothing had prepared them for what they found there. The hospital was little more than a dumping ground for wounded and dying soldiers. They lay on makeshift beds packed together in the most filthy conditions. Altogether there were 6.5km (4 miles) of beds in corridors swarming with rats, and where **cholera** and other terrible diseases spread like wildfire.

BOULOGNE FISHWOMEN CARRYING THE LUGGAGE OF THE NURSES FOR THE EAST.

▶ **French fisherwomen carry the nurses' luggage as they make their way to the French port of Marseilles. From here they would catch a ship to Turkey.**

Sea travel

Today people can fly from London to Turkey in just a few hours. But in Victorian times people had to travel overland or by sea. The journey by sea could be very rough and take about two weeks, depending on the weather. Even the largest passenger and troop ships were much smaller than many of the ships we see today. Many were powered by steam engines, but some still had sails and were powered by the wind.

The lady with the lamp

At first, Florence and her nurses were ignored by the doctors at Scutari. The only place where they could do some useful work when they first arrived was the hospital kitchen. For the first few days they cleaned it up and started making some decent food so that at least the wounded soldiers could be fed properly.

To the rescue

From mid-November 1854, huge numbers of wounded soldiers started pouring into Scutari. The doctors simply could not cope with so many and, at the end of the month, they finally asked Florence and her nurses for their help. Immediately they set to work. Floors were scrubbed clean and bedlinen was washed. The nurses also ordered new clothes, food, soap and medicines. With fresh supplies, they were able to dress the soldiers' terrible wounds and give them medicines.

Florence became known as the 'lady with the lamp' because she would walk through the wards at night carrying a lantern to check that everything was in order and to comfort the sick, the wounded and the dying. She was incredibly impressed by the soldiers' bravery. She talked to them, wrote letters for them and made sure they were treated with respect.

▶ Florence's famous lamp is now kept at the Florence Nightingale Museum in London. Its soft glow was very reassuring to the wounded soldiers in Scutari.

▲ Within days of starting their work at Scutari, Florence and her nurses had transformed the hospital's wards so that they were clean and efficiently run. This painting shows a ward at Scutari in about 1856.

Too much work

Within just a few weeks, the conditions in the hospital had improved greatly. Florence sometimes worked for 24 hours a day, for days on end. All this hard work took its toll, and in May 1855 she collapsed from exhaustion and fell dangerously ill herself from fever. She nearly died, but was saved by a devoted nurse who helped her to recover. Florence's health would never be the same again and illness would bother her for the rest of her life.

Mary Seacole

Mary Seacole was born in Kingston, Jamaica in 1805. In 1854 she travelled to England and then on to the Crimea. She worked there as a nurse and, despite having no formal training, became famous for her work helping wounded soldiers in the **Crimean War**. She became known as 'Mother Seacole' amongst the soldiers. Unlike Florence Nightingale, however, she was soon forgotten when she returned to England at the end of the war. It wasn't until many years later that she was remembered again. She died in 1881.

A grateful nation

On 30 March 1856 a treaty was signed and peace was declared. The **Crimean War** had ended. Three months later, Florence Nightingale left Scutari and travelled through France on her way back to England. By now she was a national **heroine** and great celebrations were planned for her return. But she wanted to avoid all the fuss. Travelling under another name, she slipped unrecognized into England and travelled north to Lea Hurst in Derbyshire.

Royal support

Back home once more, Florence received sack loads of fan mail and the legend of her incredible work grew and grew. One of the most important letters she received came from Queen Victoria, who wrote inviting Florence to visit her at Balmoral Castle in Scotland. Florence told the queen all about the poor treatment of the soldiers in the Crimea and how important it was to improve army hospitals.

▼ Even before Florence returned to England at the end of the war, her name was known all over the country. Souvenirs, like these china figures of her, were made to celebrate her achievement.

Changes are made

Queen Victoria agreed to support Florence's **campaign** to change the army health service. A **Royal Commission** was set up in 1857 and the person put in charge was Florence's friend, Sidney Herbert. Florence gathered as much information as she could, and by the end of the year she had written a huge, thousand-page report. Her main message was that soldiers were dying from **neglect** – terrible living conditions, poor food and clothing and bad medical treatments.

Eventually the Commission agreed to make most of the changes recommended by Florence. Army **barracks** were rebuilt and a number of new military hospitals opened. A new army medical college was opened at Chatham in Kent. Soon the death rate among soldiers in the British Army was halved.

▶ A photograph of Florence and her nurses in 1886 at the Training School she helped to set up in 1860.

The Nightingale nurses

After her work on military hospitals, Florence was asked to look at non-military hospitals. In 1860 she set up the Nightingale Training School for Nurses at St Thomas's Hospital in London. It was a training school for nurses where they learned about medicines and the importance of **hygiene** in hospitals. This was a time of great advances in medical treatments and soon hospitals from all over the world were asking for nurses trained at the school. Nurses are still trained there today.

The final years

Florence spent much of her time travelling the country and gathering information for her **campaign** for hospital improvements. She wrote endless reports and letters to as many important people as she could, to drum up support for her cause. In 1860 she wrote a very important book called *Notes on Nursing*. This laid down the rules for modern nursing. It has been translated into other languages and remained in use for many years.

Confined to bed

Florence was exhausted and growing weaker as the years passed. She was forced to go to bed for days on end. But even from there she continued her work. A terrible blow came in August 1861 when her great friend and supporter, Sidney Herbert, collapsed and died.

▲ This was Florence's bedroom at Claydon House in Buckinghamshire. Her sister, Parthenope, had married Sir Henry Verney in 1858. Claydon House was his family home.

By now Florence was so influential that she became known as 'The Commander-in-Chief'. Politicians and other important people came flocking to ask her advice. For the remaining 50 years of her life, she was unable to walk and had to spend much of the time in bed or resting in a chair. She was nearly blind for the nine years before her death. In 1907 she was awarded the **Order of Merit** by King Edward VII. This was one of the highest honours in the land and Florence became the first woman to receive it.

A simple funeral

Three years later, on 13 August 1910, Florence Nightingale died peacefully in her sleep. She was 90 years old when she died. Always hating fuss and bother, she had given strict instructions in her will that she was to be buried quietly in Hampshire, near her old family home at Embley. A small stone cross marks her grave inscribed with the words 'F.N. Born 1820. Died 1910'.

▶ **This is Florence's Order of Merit, which was given to her by the king in 1907.**

Awards and honours

The Order of Merit was founded in 1902 by King Edward VII. It is awarded to people who have done very special work in science, art or writing. There are only ever 24 members of the Order at any one time. Florence Nightingale was the first woman to be awarded the honour and it was to be another 58 years before another woman received it.

Florence's influence today

Florence Nightingale was a very modest woman who always hated a fuss being made over her. But the incredible work this extraordinary woman did meant that she became one of the most famous and powerful people in the country. She never married and never had any children, but after her death she was missed by the thousands of people she had helped for so many years. The name of Florence Nightingale has continued to be famous nearly 100 years after her death, and will probably remain famous for many more years to come.

Fighting for her beliefs

Florence Nightingale was a determined, intelligent woman who knew, ever since she was a girl, that she wanted to help other less fortunate people.

She was born into a rich family and could have spent the rest of her life in great comfort and without a care in the world. For many years, her own family tried to stop her doing the things she wanted, because women in those days were not supposed to behave as she did. But she fought against the opposition of her family. She chose not to follow the way most people thought women should lead their lives. She broke free and showed just how much women were capable of.

▲ This photograph of Florence in her old age was taken in 1891, when she was 71 years old.

Modern nursing

Florence's incredibly brave work during the **Crimean War** meant that she returned to England a national **heroine**. Her work after that was even more important. She changed the way in which British soldiers were regarded by their officers, so that they were treated with respect.

During World War I, which broke out four years after Florence's death, nurses were trained to do many of the things that Florence herself had done at Scutari, such as write letters for soldiers.

She completely changed the way sick and poor people were treated and the way hospitals were run. Hospitals were transformed into clean, efficient organizations in which patients could expect to receive the best care. Thanks to her, nurses are now trained to very high standards. Florence's pioneering work forms the basis of modern nursing today.

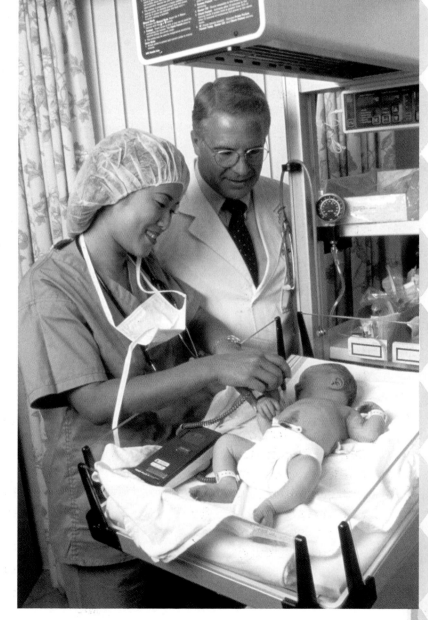

▶ A baby receives treatment using clean, modern equipment in a hospital today.

Glossary

bacteria tiny, microscopic germs that can cause disease

barracks building or group of buildings where soldiers live

campaign activity by one or more people, designed to influence other people and achieve a goal

cholera serious infection of the stomach that, unless treated quickly, can lead to death

Crimean War war between Russia on one side and Turkey, Britain and France on the other. It was fought between 1853–56.

drunkard person who is often or always drunk

estate large area of privately owned land, usually in the country

governess woman teacher to a family

heroine woman with heroic qualities such as great bravery

honeymoon holiday taken by a newly married couple

hygiene clean and healthy practices, like washing your hands

industry industries make goods for sale, often using machinery

influenza highly infectious disease causing fever, aches and pains and sometimes death

inherit receive property or money from someone else, often through a will

journalist person who reports and writes about news stories

neglect failure to give care, attention or time to someone or something

nervous breakdown mental illness, often caused by exhaustion or worry

Order of Merit award for outstanding public service, founded in 1902

philosophy from the ancient Greek word for 'lover of knowledge'. It is the study of ideas, the nature of human life and behaviour.

public health service health treatment of citizens in hospitals and clinics

rickets disease, mainly found in children, caused by a poor diet leading to weak and deformed bones

Royal Commission official investigation into the country's laws or some other important matter. It is set up by the king or queen on the advice of the prime minister.

superintendent person who directs and manages an organization, such as a hospital

territory area of land, often part of a country

Timeline

1820   Florence Nightingale is born

1821–29 Greek War of Independence from Turkey

1837   Victoria becomes Queen of Great Britain

1853   Crimean War breaks out between Russia and Turkey

1854   Florence Nightingale travels to the Crimea with a team of nurses

1856   Treaty of Paris ends the Crimean War

1860   Nightingale Training School for Nurses opens in London

1864   Red Cross Society is founded in Geneva

1865   Louis Pasteur publishes his germ theory of disease

1867   Joseph Lister describes his use of antiseptics to reduce infections

1901   Queen Victoria dies. Edward VII becomes king.

1907   Florence Nightingale is awarded the Order of Merit by Edward VII

1910   Florence Nightingale dies

Further reading & websites

Florence Nightingale, John Malam (Heinemann Library, 2001)

Florence Nightingale, Philip Ardagh (Macmillan Children's, 1999)

Florence Nightingale (Wayland, 1999)

Life and Work in 19th Century Britain, Rachel Hames (Heinemann History, 1995)

Heinemann Explore – an online resource from Heinemann.
For Key Stage 2 history go to *www.heinemannexplore.co.uk*.

www.florence-nightingale.co.uk – Florence Nightingale Museum website

http://womenshistory.about.com/cs/nightingale/

Places to visit

Florence Nightingale Museum, London

East Wellow Church, Romsey, Hampshire (where Florence Nightingale is buried)

Claydon House, Buckinghamshire

Lea Hurst, Matlock, Derbyshire

Embley House, Romsey, Hampshire (now a school)

Index